thelwell country

thelwell country

METHUEN

A Methuen Paperback

THELWELL COUNTRY

ISBN 0 417 01080 X

First published 1959 by Methuen & Co. Ltd
reprinted 1964
First paperback edition published 1970 by Eyre
Methuen Ltd
reprinted five times
This (Magnum) reprint 1978
Reprinted 1980

This edition published 1982 by Methuen London Ltd
11 New Fetter Lane, London EC4P 4EE
Reprinted 1984, 1986

Made and printed in Great Britain by
Richard Clay (The Chaucer Press) Ltd
Bungay, Suffolk

for
THOSE WHO ENJOY THE COUNTRY LIFE

Most of the drawings in this book originally appeared in *Punch*; some in the *News Chronicle*. The artist is indebted to the Proprietors of *Punch* and to the Editor of the *News Chronicle* for permission to publish them here.

contents

" That's *one* Christmas present she won't break in a hurry."

foreword

HUMOROUS artists used to represent the countryside—a few unfortunately still do—as a weird backward region inhabited by unbelievably yokelly yokels and visited by townspeople who were frightened of cows and made fools of themselves with unfamiliar objects like guns and horses. Norman Thelwell never patronises. He knows the country, and assumes that you and I know it too. Thelwell country is real country. Surprising things happen in it, of course; man and nature, unaided by Thelwell's imagination, do not often combine to produce such happy contretemps as those on pages 35 and 51. But always, as in all good farce, the background, the setting, is real, solid, convincing.

Accuracy in detail adds the pleasure of recognition to Thelwell's wildest fancies. He is not content just to draw "seagulls". Having myself an amateur interest in birds I am entranced by the overcrowded island on page 72, and have even tried to carry out a razorbill count with a magnifying glass. There are very properly, no avocets on this rocky crag, but Thelwell could not resist introducing a couple—no, three—no, I'm sorry, there are two more near the door, making five in all—into that pleasant kitchen on page 19. I am not knowledgeable about farming matters, but I do not doubt that the sheep in this book are not mere "sheep" but belong to specific breeds readily identifiable by the expert. Thelwell's popularity with country people, with the farmers and the pony-club members at whom he laughs is due to the fact that he *knows* what he is laughing at. For the rest of us, less directly attacked and ignorant, perhaps, of some of the finer points, it is enough that his ideas are so funny and he draws so well.

There is so much in this present collection to please the eye. Look at the church roof on page 26, the farm buildings on page 14, the cedar tree—and never mind the jokes for the moment—on page 23, the trawler (or is it a drifter? The uncertainty is mine, not the artist's) on page 39. Is not that a warm and grateful stackyard on page 30? It is by no means *necessary* for a humorous drawing to be in itself a pleasant thing to look at, or to be enriched by attractive detail. Much modern comic art aims at the exclusion of everything that is not intrinsic to the joke, and some highly successful and satisfying results (together with a lot of thin rubbish) have been achieved by this insistence on the utmost brevity of "statement". But

9

numour cannot, thank goodness, be controlled by theories or confined within dogmatic limits; Thelwell's finds its proper expression "in the round"—in a recognisable world where bulls have mass and momentum, stone walls have knobbliness and texture, and combine harvesters squelch heavily through genuine mud. When a humorous artist provides visual enjoyment as well as a good laugh, I do not feel that one ought to complain.

About the quality of Thelwell's humorous ideas, as distinct from his drawing, I don't propose to argue. Humour is an individual thing, and no man will submit to being lectured on what is funny and what is not. If I were to draw the reader's attention to the drawings on pages 36, 62 and 74 as perfect examples of Thelwell's delicious, unstrained, beautifully timed humour, he would very likely draw mine to the wilder absurdities on pages 14, 51 and 95. Not that I should mind. I should be quite willing, in Round Two, to play the pony-tail joke on page 61 or the tramp on page 84 against the reader's championship of the rout of the picnickers on page 34. But I don't see where it would lead us.

There are six avocets on page 19, by the way. I quite failed to see the biggest of the lot—in flight up there under the beams.   H. F. ELLIS

thelwell country

" It's in the Green Belt, of course."

" There you are! Fifty per cent nylon."

" Lot 64. What am I bid ? "

As a result of myxomatosis, foxes are
becoming as savage as wolves . . .

and birds, owing to the Protection of Birds Act, are losing their fear of man; so that . . .

seems likely to become complicated.

" I thought the recession wasn't supposed to affect us ? "

" If we don't sell some of our surplus coal stocks soon—we'll have
to consider throwing the place open to the public."

" Vicar says can you let 'im 'ave a nice bit of wheat . . .

". . . for the 'Arvest Festival ? "

"On account of the widespread floods we will omit
the verse about soft refreshing rain"

I said " If you want a job doing properly,
you've got to do it yourself."

"It'll be the most disastrous year I've ever
known if this lot catches fire."

" My wife's just the same. Now she wants a spin dryer."

" Quick Chaps! . . . .

. . . . Here comes the British Travel Association Photographer."

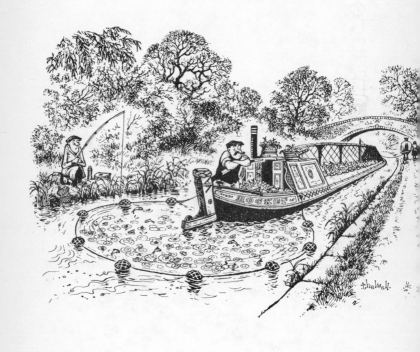

" Know why they put glass bottoms in tankards son ? "

its horses

" It's so sordid Charles—having to meet like this."

" The trouble with you city dwellers is that you
just don't understand the farmers' . . .

. . . point of view."

The Body Beautiful
WHAT THREE MONTHS RIDING CAN DO

Before—

The Body Beautiful

—After

" It's no use making a noise like that!
You've *been* blooded once."

Humane Meet

" Go ahead! Now tell me *that's* not the Horse of the Year! "

" She just asked me if she could have a few friends in to watch the
International Horse Show."

" I'll just try to get him to say a few words."

" Here comes Charlie! Let's have a rubber of bridge."

" Now we mustn't lose our temper Wendy. Perhaps we'll be good
enough for the gymkhana next year."

its bird life

" All right Charlie! Send them up."

" I warned you against fish paste sandwiches."

" Where do we set up the hide ? "

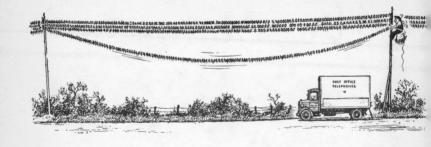

its nomads

" It's their simplicity that I envy."

its trade

" It's nice to see that modern sales techniques have at last . . . .

. . . reached our village."

" Lovely firewood."

" Who's there ? "

and, of course, its people

TORSO